The Secrets Animal Flight

NIC BISHOP

Houghton Mifflin Company

Boston

The author wishes to thank Cameron Smith.

www.houghtonmifflinbooks.com

The text of this book is Meridien.
Book design: Lisa Diercks

Library of Congress Cataloging-in-Publication Data
Bishop, Nic.
The secrets of animal flight / by Nic Bishop.
p. cm.
Summary: In text and photographs, presents birds, insects, bats, and other flying animals.
HC ISBN-10: 0-395-77848-4 PB ISBN-10: 0-618-80904-X
1. Animal flight—Juvenile literature. [1.Animal flight.] I. Title.
QP310.F5B57   1997
591.1'852—dc20 96-23131 CIP AC

HC ISBN-13: 978-0-395-77848-7
PA ISBN-13: 978-0-618-80904-2

Printed in Singapore
TWP 10 9 8 7 6 5 4

Why Fly?

Flying animals are everywhere. Butterflies dance through the park and sea gulls soar by the ocean. Even in the middle of the night, moths flutter through the darkness while bats zip and zoom trying to catch them.

In some parts of the world, really strange animals take to the air — flying frogs, snakes, lizards, squirrels, even fish! But, like this flying gecko from Burma, these animals can glide only a short way, using flaps of skin. They don't have proper wings and can't really fly. Birds, bats, and insects are the true fliers. Only they have fully mastered the air.

But why fly? It looks fun, but the real reason is it's useful. First, it's a great way to get around. A non-flying animal has to slosh through streams, clamber over fences, and climb steep hills, all the while on the lookout out for bigger animals that might eat it. But with wings, an animal can fly straight to its destination.

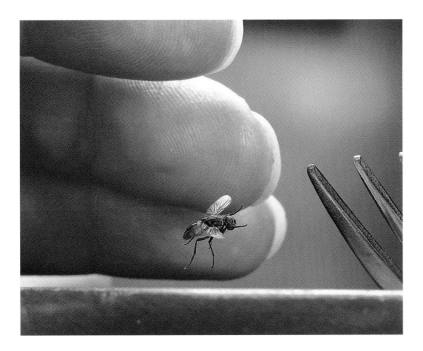

Flight is also a handy means of escape. If a bird or insect is attacked on the ground, it can lift off to safety, like the fly above. Flying animals can also raise their families in nests, high off the ground and safe from earthbound enemies. Another bonus is that fliers can get to food that others can't, like this macaw munching papaw in a treetop.

But flying has drawbacks. It takes lots of energy. Energy comes from food, so flying animals spend lots of time looking for things to eat, and not just anything will do. They need energy-rich foods like seeds, fruit, nectar, and meat. That's why most birds don't eat grasses or leaves. These foods don't give enough energy.

Flying animals also have to be lightweight. Heavy animals need too much muscle power to take off. Even a large eagle only weighs about 12 pounds. A 150-pound person would need flight muscles up to 6 feet deep and wings as wide as 120 feet from tip to tip to fly!

Staying Up

Flying looks easy. A swallow or a dragonfly swooping across the sky seems to just float in the air. What holds them up?

The secret of flight is the wing. When air blows over a wing it creates a force called *lift*. Lift is what pulls a wing up, lifting an animal into the air. But

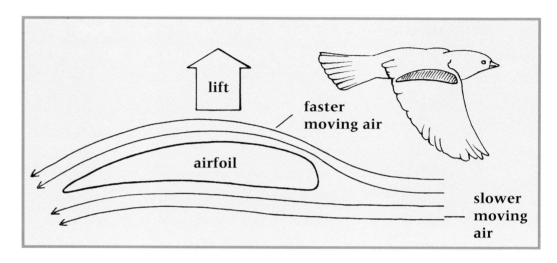

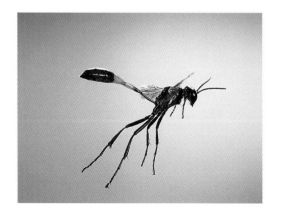

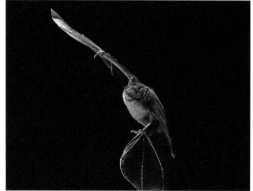

lift depends on the wing having the right shape. That shape is an *airfoil*. Birds, bats, and most insects have wings that are airfoils. Airplane wings have the same shape and work the same way as animal wings to give lift.

The top surface of an airfoil is curved, while the bottom is flatter. Air passing over the curved top of an airfoil has to travel farther than the air underneath, so it moves faster to keep up with the air moving under the wing. This fast-moving air pulls away from the wing, causing suction that pulls the wing up.

You can see how this works. Hold the end of a thin strip of newspaper in front of your mouth, letting the paper hang down. Now blow over the curved top and see what happens. The fast-moving air causes the paper to lift. The harder you blow, the higher the paper will rise. In just the same way, the faster an animal or airplane wing moves forward through the air, the more lift it makes.

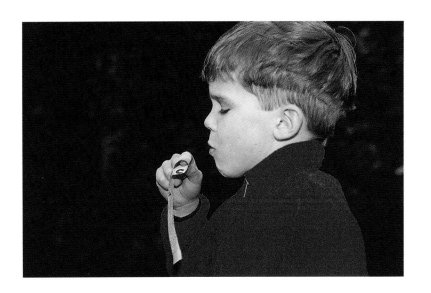

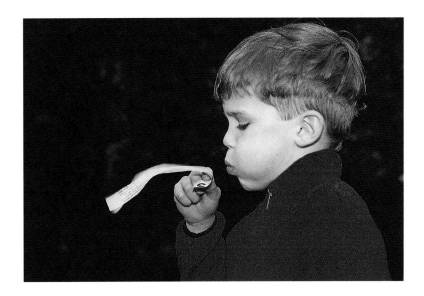

The Feathered Wing

Birds fly higher and faster than any other animal. Airline pilots have spotted whooper swans at 27,000 feet. Pigeons can fly for hundreds of miles at more than 50 miles per hour, and falcons can dive at 200 miles per hour!

A bird is custom-designed for flight. It has hollow bones for lightness and special air sacs to help move air through its lungs so it can fly fast without getting out of breath. Its chest also contains powerful muscles to flap the wings.

But a bird's most important flying equipment is its wings and feathers. A bird's wing is really its arm. It has muscles and bones like your arm, and bends at the shoulder, elbow, and wrist. But unlike your hand, a bird's hand is long compared to its arm, and many of its fingers are joined together.

Feathers growing on the bird's arm and hand give the wing its shape. Small feathers, called covert feathers, cover the front of the wing;

behind these are larger feathers, called flight feathers, which support and propel the bird in the air. The flight feathers on the arm part of the wing are called secondaries and tertiaries, while those on the hand part of the wing are called primaries.

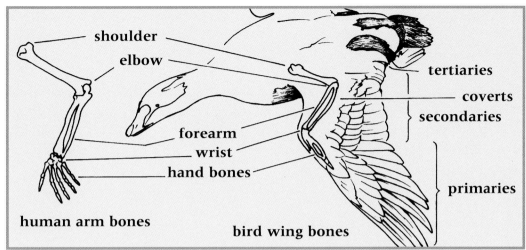

shoulder
elbow
tertiaries
coverts
secondaries
forearm
wrist
hand bones
primaries
human arm bones
bird wing bones

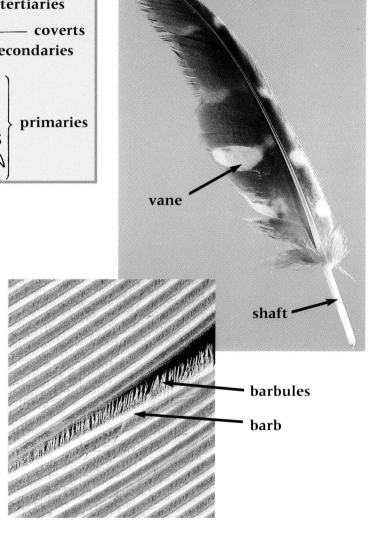

vane
shaft
barbules
barb

Feathers may look simple, but they're really very complicated. Each one can have more than a million tiny parts. In the middle of the feather is a shaft that supports a flat vane made of smaller shafts called barbs. Each barb is fastened to the one next to it by even smaller shafts called barbules. These barbules have hooks that stick the barbs together like Velcro. So if a bird damages its feather and two barbs split apart, it just strokes them together with its beak and they hook up again. A bird spends a lot of time each day checking and grooming each feather so it's always ready for flight.

The Downstroke

When a bird moves its wings downward, in a downstroke, its flight feathers do two things: they give propulsion, or push, to move the bird forward, and lift to pull it up. Propulsion comes from the primary feathers on the hand part of the wing. They act like propellers, moving the bird along as it flaps its wings. The blades of an airplane propeller are airfoils that spin around, pulling air from in front of the airplane and pushing it out behind. This backward blast of air drives the airplane forward. Of course, a bird's primary feathers can't spin like airplane propellers, but they do the same job.

To see how this happens, first look at the single primary feather from a chickadee. Notice how the vane is wider behind the shaft than it is in front. Now look at what happens to the chicka-

primary feather in propeller shape

chickadee primary feather

front vane

rear vane

shaft

dee's primary feathers as it flies. As the wings move down, wind pushes against the wide rear vane of each primary, twisting the front vane down into the shape of a propeller blade. As they sweep down, these miniature blades bite into the air, moving the air backward and the bird forward.

Most of the lift comes from the secondary and tertiary flight feathers on the arm part of the wing. They and the covert feathers give this part of the wing its airfoil shape. Lift is created from air blowing over these feathers as the bird flies.

So while a bird's hands act like airplane propellers to give propulsion, its arms act like airplane wings to give lift. Different birds have different size hands or arms, depending on how they fly. Flappers like chickadees have large hands for propulsion to dart between branches. Gliders like hawks have longer arms for lift to carry them high in the sky.

The Upstroke

A bird gets most of its flight power from the downstroke. For the upstroke, the wings need to be lifted with as little drag as possible. Drag is the pull of the wind on the bird's feathers, which slows it down.

You can see two things the chickadee does to make it easier to lift its wings. First it draws the tips of its wings back and toward its body a little. This folds the primary feathers like a half-closed fan, so the wing tips meet less resistance from the air as they move up. Then, as the primaries come

up, the wind pushing against their wide rear vanes twists them open like the slats of a venetian blind. This lets air flow between the feathers, so there's less drag.

The chickadee also wastes no time raising its wings so it's ready for the next downstroke. It lifts the arm parts of its wings first, then flicks its wrists to snap the primary feathers above its head once more.

In real life, a bird flaps its wings too fast for us to see all the movements. A chickadee beats its wings almost thirty times every second. Each beat is also a little different, as a bird is always changing the shape of its wings to steer through the air. It can even move single wing feathers to alter its flight path. To do all this and flap at the same time, a chickadee's brain has to work like a high-speed flight computer!

Taking Off and Landing

It's amazing how quickly a bird takes off, especially when compared to an airplane. An airplane has to roar down a long runway before air is blowing across its wings fast enough to lift it from the ground. Yet most birds become airborne with a single flap.

A bird's secret is to use its legs and wings together. It leaps into the air, like this starling, while pushing down hard with both wings.

But some heavier birds take off more like airplanes, running to build up speed. Swans, for example, run across water flapping their wings for a long time before they climb into the sky.

Taking off is a lot of effort, but at least it's not

as dangerous as landing. A bird has to slow down just the right amount before it touches down, and it takes a lot of skill. Young birds often shoot past their perches and crash into the bushes before they finally get it right.

To land, a bird tilts its body up and spreads out its wings and tail feathers like a parachute. It can also slow down by flapping its wings so they push against the air. This is what the parrot is doing. At the last instant, the bird stretches out both legs to take the shock of landing. Birds that land on water have it easier — they use their feet as skis to skid to a halt.

Gliding and Soaring

Flying is hard work, but a bird doesn't have to flap its wings to stay in the air. It can glide.

When a bird glides, it holds its wings out motionless and points its body slightly down. Gravity pulls the bird toward the earth, but air rushing over its wings gives lift, so the bird drops gently. If the bird starts high enough, it can glide for miles, but eventually it will need to flap its wings to climb again.

Sometimes birds use air currents to carry them up without flapping their wings. When sunlight heats open ground, currents of warm air called

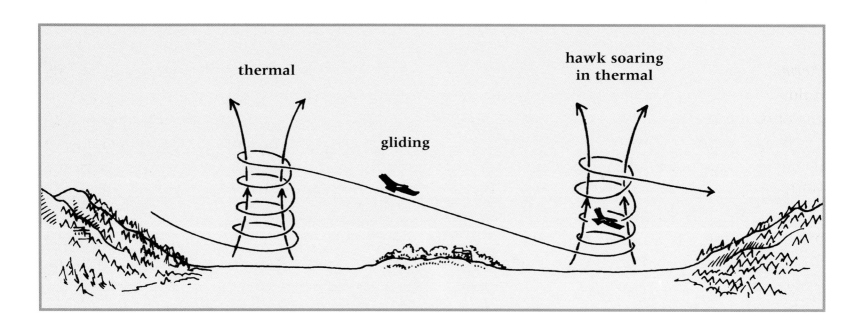

thermal

gliding

hawk soaring
in thermal

thermals rise from the earth's surface. If a bird holds out its wings and circles around in these currents, it can climb with the rising air.

Using air currents this way is called *soaring.* Eagles, hawks, and vultures are expert soarers. With their long wings they can climb higher than 20,000 feet. After getting a free lift from one thermal, a bird can glide off to another. It can travel for miles and hardly ever flap its wings.

The world's greatest glider is the wandering albatross, shown in the photograph. Its wings, which stretch 11 feet from tip to tip, are the longest of any gliding bird. The wandering albatross doesn't use thermals, but it soars and glides on the winds that blow over the oceans around Antarctica. Carried by the wind, it travels around the world many times during its life. It lands on the sea to eat or rest, and only touches ground to nest. Since birds have been known to crash into boats, sailors believe the wandering albatross glides so easily that it drops off to sleep in the air!

Bats

Bats are the only mammals that can fly. Their wings have the same bones as a human arm, but with four very long fingers — each almost as long as the bat's body. In fact, a bat is nearly all wings. The skin that makes up the wing surface stretches all the way from the bat's fingers to the ankles on its back legs.

By waggling its fingers and legs, a bat can fold

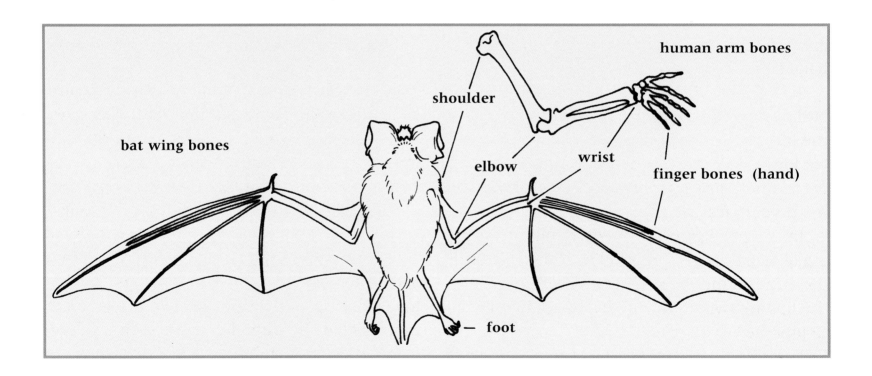

or stretch its wings into any shape. Walking isn't so easy, though, when your legs are attached to your wings. A bat can't stand up, and has to shuffle along the ground using its wrists and elbows. Vampire bats crawl very well this way so they can sneak up on sleeping animals to drink their blood, but most bats spend little time on the ground. They're either flying or hanging upside down by their feet.

To fly, a bat flaps its wings like a bird. Like a bird, the arm part of the bat's wing gives most of the lift, and the hand part of the wing drives the bat forward. As the wings move down, each hand twists into a propeller blade shape, working like the primary feathers of the bird.

In the photograph, the bat's hands are working like propellers. This bat is near the end of the downstroke and the front edges of its wings near the tips are twisted in. The hands cut into the air to pull the bat forward.

During the upstroke the bat needs to avoid drag, so it partly folds its wings. The bat also turns its hands so the palms face forward. This might help — scientists aren't sure — give an extra push forward when the wings snap back up.

Even without feathers, bats fly very well. They can hover in one spot and zoom along at 30 miles an hour. Bats are also very successful, with almost 1,000 types worldwide. The largest bat, called the flying fox, has wings five feet long from tip to tip. The smallest bat — sometimes called the bumblebee bat — has a body that is only an inch long.

Aero-bat-ics After Dark

Bats perform amazing aerobatics. Because air can't leak through a skin-covered wing as it can through a feather-covered wing, bats twist and turn in the air more sharply than birds.

What's more amazing is that bats can perform all their maneuvers in total darkness. Bats can see well in the light, but at night they use another way to "see." This is called *echolocation.*

Echolocation uses sound. As a bat flies along it opens its mouth and gives out lots of short, loud squeaks. At the same time, it listens to the echoes that bounce back from objects the noise hits. The echoes from nearby objects come back quicker and louder than those from faraway objects. The echoes from a hard tree trunk also sound different than those from the soft wings of a flying moth. So by listening carefully the bat gets a "picture" of its surroundings. Some bats can even "see" objects as thin as a human hair!

Using echolocation, bats are expert insect hunters. The bat shown on the next page has just located a cricket by following the echoes that bounce off the insect's body. Their super-sensitive ears can even hear the sound of a caterpillar's jaws munching on a leaf. Bats also hunt insects in midair, zeroing in on their favorite ones. A bat can't grab an insect with its hands — it's too busy using them to fly — but it can use a wing tip to flip one to its mouth. Sometimes the bat also flicks its tail under its body as a handy pocket to hold its dinner.

Bats love fast food — a little brown bat may catch 600 mosquitoes in an hour — and by the end of the night it can gulp down a third of its own body weight. A bat needs all that food for energy — the heart of a flying bat can beat 1,000 times a minute, more than ten times faster than your heartbeat!

The Insect Flying Machine

An insect's wing is one of the lightest structures in nature. It has no bone or muscle. Instead, the wing is made of thin layers of cutin, an amazingly tough material that also makes up an insect's hard outer skin. A network of veins gives the wing extra strength and support.

front wing

thorax

wing vein

hind wing

The wings are powered by muscles in the thorax, the middle section of an insect's body. Ounce for ounce they are the most powerful muscles known in nature. They flap the wings of flies and bees about 200 times per second, though some midges and wasps beat their wings an amazing 1,000 times per second, more than ten times faster than any bird. To handle all the wear and tear, the joint between an insect's wing and its body is very strong and elastic, otherwise it would wear out.

Most insects fly using two pairs of wings. The two front wings and two back wings can be seen on the dragonfly at right. But often the wings are joined together or overlap so they work as a single pair, as in butterflies and wasps. In beetles like the ladybug, the front wings are hard covers, called *elytra,* which protect the back wings when

they're not in use. This makes the beetle's body tough, but it also makes the beetle's take-offs clumsy. It has to work to unfold its wings from under the elytra. That's why ladybugs and other beetles sometimes tumble over trying to get airborne.

All insects have trouble taking off unless their flight muscles are warm enough. Like your muscles, they don't work well when they're cold. So on chilly mornings, insects warm up before heading into the sky. Butterflies open their wings as solar panels to absorb heat from the sun. Other insects heat their flight muscles by vibrating them, just as you can warm your muscles by shivering. After a few moments, the insect puts its wings into gear and zooms away.

Nature's Helicopters

This wasp shows how most insects fly. At the start of the downstroke both wings are above and behind its head. Then it sweeps its wings down and forward, similar to birds and bats. Air passing over the wings gives the insect lift.

But during the upstroke, insect wings behave very differently from those of most other animals. If you look closely at the last three photographs you can see that as the wings travel up and back, they twist upside down. This neat trick means the

wings get as much lift from the upstroke as from the downstroke—birds and bats get most of their flight power from the downstroke.

Insects are nature's helicopters. You can think of their wings as helicopter rotor blades. As the wings flap back and forth they constantly pull air from in front of the insect and push it out behind. To hover like a helicopter, the insect tilts its body up and fans its wings horizontal to the ground. Air is blown straight down and the insect hangs in one spot. To fly forward, it tilts its body and wings forward so air is blown back, forcing the insect along. Hummingbirds are the only other animals that come close to flying like insects. They too can flip their wings upside down and hover.

One of nature's niftiest helicopters is the housefly. As it darts through your bedroom it can stop in midair, hover, twirl its body around, loop the loop, and then do a cartwheel to land upside down on the ceiling. Try that with a helicopter!

Zooming and Gliding

For their size, insects are speedy. Some dragonflies, bees, and wasps are thought to reach 45 miles an hour. Insects are also strong. A bumblebee can double in weight as it collects pollen and nectar. Yet it flies the load back home easily.

Bumblebees, like all insects, use a lot of energy to fly. But because insects are so small they can go a long way on what seems like very little. A bumblebee can travel 2,000 miles on just one teaspoon of nectar! Of course each flower gives only the tiniest amount of nectar — just about enough to keep a bumblebee going for a minute — so it must keep feeding and collecting all day. An average bumblebee may stop at more than a hundred flowers on each trip from the nest, like a car that has to stop at every gas station because each pump will only give a cupful of gas.

Some insects save energy by gliding. Dragonflies often stop beating their wings to glide a short way. Most gliders, like this heliconiid butterfly, live in the rainforest. A heliconiid's wings are long and thin, like a miniature glider aircraft. Its thorax is also small because it doesn't need powerful flight muscles. There are lots of gliding insects in the rainforest because the air there is very calm and sheltered. If you let a heliconiid butterfly go in your garden, it would immediately be blown away by the wind.

Flight of the Butterfly

A flying butterfly seems to skip and dance through the air, its body bobbing up and down with each flap of its wings. Scientists have only recently begun to discover how butterflies use their large wings in unusual ways that push and yank them through the air.

This painted lady butterfly starts with both wings pressed together above its head. When it opens them, as shown in the first photograph, something curious happens. Rather than a simple downstroke, the wings peel apart like two pages of a book. The front edges of the wings part first, and air rushes in from in front of the butterfly to

fill the space between the opening wings. This gives the painted lady a little tug and lifts it in the air.

After the wings open out, they give lift the same way as the wings of other animals. But at the start of the upstroke, illustrated by the fourth photograph, the butterfly may use its wings to get another tug through the air. You can see the butterfly's body tilt up. As the front edges of the wings open, the back edges under the body stay closed. This may help pull the butterfly forward and up in a manner similar to the downstroke. The butterfly may get another small push forward when its wings clap together again, as shown in the last photograph.

The large wings of a butterfly also make great getaway devices. When a butterfly feeds it often keeps its wings open, warming them in the sun. But if it sees you sneaking up it will close them. The butterfly watches carefully and, before you get too close, snaps its wings open again. Both wings push straight down on the air like huge paddles and the butterfly shoots straight up like a rocket. Before you can blink, it's skipping safely into the sky.

Mysteries of Flight

E ven though humans have studied flying animals for hundreds of years, we still have many things to learn. One mystery is the huge distance birds are able to fly when they migrate to warmer countries for the winter. The birds in this photograph are called godwits and they have flown 9,000 miles from Alaska and Siberia to New Zealand. They stop on their journey to feed

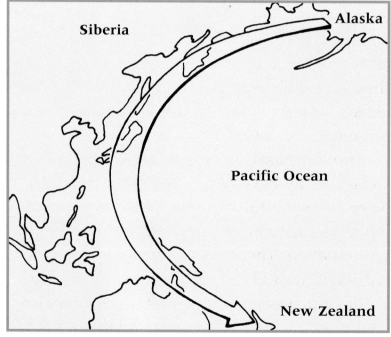

and refuel, but when they cross seas they just keep going, flying day and night to get to the other side. Some birds fly 2,000 miles nonstop. How do they do it? Even the tiny ruby-throated hummingbird — weighing little more than a dime — crosses 500 miles of sea between the United States and Mexico!

Insects also make long migrations. Each fall, millions of monarch butterflies from the eastern United States and Canada fly to Mexico. A few even travel 2,000 miles, but what's more fantastic is that every year, all the butterflies fly to the same tiny region in Mexico. Some people think they find their way by feeling the earth's magnetism, as if they have a compass in their bodies, but no one really knows.

Another puzzle about insects is how they fly so fast. Many have wings that seem too small to be really powerful, and some have such strange wings it's a wonder their owners get off the ground at all. These insects must be using tricks we don't know about yet.

To help answer these questions, scientists use computers, wind tunnels, and high-speed pho-

tographs, like the ones in this book. They have filmed flying birds with x-rays to watch their skeletons move. One scientist has even tried building a robot model of a moth wing to see how it flaps. Discoveries are made every year, but it will be a long time before we know everything about how animals move through the air. In all of nature, few things are so mysterious and beautiful as flight.

Further Reading

Cole, Joanna. *A Bird's Body.* Photographs by Jerome Wexler. New York: Morrow Jr. Books, 1982.

Earle, Ann. *Zipping, Zapping, Zooming Bats.* New York: HarperCollins Children's Books, 1995.

Freedman, Russell. *How Birds Fly.* New York: Holiday House, 1977.

Halton, Cheryl Mays. *Those Amazing Bats.* Minneapolis, Minn.: Dillon Press, Inc., 1991.

Kaufmann, John. *Birds are Flying.* New York: Crowell, 1979.

Lavies, Bianca. *Monarch Butterflies: Mysterious Travelers.* New York: Dutton Children's Books, 1992.

Parker, Steve, and Jane Parker. *Migration.* New York: Gloucester Press, 1992.

Patent, Dorothy Hinshaw. *Feathers.* Photographs by William Munoz. New York: Cobblehill Books, 1992.

Pringle, Laurence. *Batman: Exploring the World of Bats.* Illustrated by Merlin D. Tuttle. New York: Scholastic Inc., 1991.

Ricciuti, Edward R. *Birds.* Woodbridge, Conn.: Blackbirch Press, 1993.

Snedden, Robert. *What Is a Bird?* San Francisco: Sierra Club Books for Children, 1993.

Tesar, Jenny. *Insects.* Woodbridge, Conn.: Blackbirch Press, 1993.

Walker, Ormiston H. *Experimenting with Air and Flight.* New York: Franklin Watts, 1989.

Award-winning author and photographer **Nic Bishop** is known for his outstanding stop-action wildlife photographs. He has been the photographer for many successful books for children, including *Red-Eyed Tree Frog* by Joy Cowell and books in Houghton Mifflin's Scientists in the Field series: *The Tarantula Scientist*, a 2004 Sibert Honor book, and *The Snake Scientist*, winner of the 2000 IRA Children's Book Award for nonfiction, both written by Sy Montgomery; and *Digging for Bird-Dinosaurs*, which he also wrote. He lives in Kalamazoo, Michigan, with his wife and many animals.